Basic Quiltmaking Techniques

for Borders and Bindings

Mimi Dietrich

Martingale
& C O M P A N Y

Bothell, Washington

Credits

President .... Nancy J. Martin
CEO/Publisher .... Daniel J. Martin
Associate Publisher .... Jane Hamada
Editorial Director............. Mary V. Green
Design and
    Production Manager ..... Cheryl Stevenson
Technical Editor........... Christine Barnes
Copy Editor .... Tina Cook
Cover Designer........... Magrit Baurecht
Text Designer .... Kay Green
Illustrator.................. Laurel Strand
Photographer .... Brent Kane

Basic Quiltmaking Techniques for
Borders and Bindings
© 1998 by Mimi Dietrich

Martingale & Company
PO Box 118
Bothell, WA 98041-0118 USA

Printed in the United States of America
03 02 01 00 99   6 5 4 3

Dedication

To Jon and Ryan. You both have grown up surrounded by quilts and quilters. You deserve a book dedicated to you!

Acknowledgments

Many, many thanks to:

My friend Carol Doak, author of *Your First Quilt Book (or it should be!)*, who inspired this series of fun books for beginners.

Ursula Reikes of Martingale & Company and Christine Barnes, who provided long-distance editorial guidance.

Linda Newson, Quilted with Care, who lovingly machine quilted projects for the book.

Barbara McMahon, who looked at the Pinwheel quilt and said "Sparkles!"

Beth Rice, who shared ideas for quilting the Pinwheel quilt.

Robbyn Robinson, who is so fabulous with color selections.

Norma Campbell and Laurie Gregg, understanding and encouraging friends.

Bob Dietrich. Thanks, Hon!

MISSION STATEMENT

WE ARE DEDICATED TO PROVIDING QUALITY PRODUCTS AND SERVICE BY WORKING TOGETHER TO INSPIRE CREATIVITY AND TO ENRICH THE LIVES WE TOUCH.

Library of Congress Cataloging-in-Publication Data
Dietrich, Mimi.
    Basic quiltmaking techniques for borders and bindings / Mimi Dietrich.
        p. cm.
    Includes bibliographical references (p.).
    ISBN 1-56477-253-5
    1. Quilting. 2. Patchwork. 3. Patchwork quilts. 4. Borders, Ornamental (Decorative arts) I. Title.
TT835.D527 1998
746.46—dc21   98-30691
                                 CIP

Contents

Foreword

Borders and bindings are such important components of your quiltmaking projects, yet the techniques that make them creative, appropriate, and well executed are often overlooked.

Mimi Dietrich is going to change all of that for you. On the following pages, she offers valuable instructions for basic borders and bindings that build on the information in *Your First Quilt Book (or it should be!)*. Mimi has vast experience teaching quiltmakers how to create borders and bindings that complement their quilts. If you learned Mimi's techniques in *Basic Quiltmaking Techniques for Hand Appliqué*, you're already familiar with her easy, step-by-step instructions, clear illustrations, and charming projects.

There is more to framing and finishing your quilts than meets the eye. Let Mimi guide you through the steps needed to create borders that enhance your quilt tops and bindings that neatly finish the edges. Six quilt projects provide you with the opportunity to try her techniques on a variety of quilt designs.

You'll want to keep this addition to your Basic Quiltmaking Techniques library handy when it's time to stitch the perfect ending to all your quilt projects.

Carol Doak

Preface

Ten years ago I wrote a book entitled *Happy Endings: Finishing the Edges of Your Quilts.* I wrote it to help quilters make and apply the binding on their quilts. *Happy Endings* has taken me on a wonderful journey through the world of quilting. I have written other books, taught classes to delightful groups in fabulous places, and met quilters from all over the world. *Happy Endings* was really only a beginning!

When Carol Doak and the editors at Martingale & Company began to develop a series of books for beginners based on Carol's *Your First Quilt Book (or it should be!)*, I was excited because I wanted to condense the basic information—the techniques I use almost every time I finish a quilt—from *Happy Endings*, combine it with border information, and produce a practical, easy-to-use book.

When I teach Happy Endings classes and we talk about bindings, we also talk about borders. Quilt borders and bindings work together. If you sew a border on your quilt properly, the edges of your quilt will not ripple and your binding will be neat. To achieve flat, straight edges, you must measure the quilt through the middle and cut the borders accordingly. Using the techniques in this book, you can easily cut and sew straight-cut borders, borders with corner squares, multiple-fabric borders, or mitered borders. Pieced borders require a little extra explanation, but they are easy to make, even for beginners.

Once you attach the borders, you can bind your quilt with straight-grain or bias strips. If you prepare the quilt edges for binding and sew carefully, your quilt will look great! This book includes the best basic information on adding borders and finishing the edges of your quilt with binding.

So please don't put this book on the shelf. Put it in a special place in your sewing area, right next to your sewing machine, so you will have the information at hand when you stitch borders or bindings on your next quilt.

When you have stitched the last stitch on your binding, smile and enjoy your accomplishment—you've finished your quilt! You've spent creative time with designs and colors you love, and you've taken pleasure in working with them. Hang the quilt on your wall and love it. Lay it over your bed and admire it. But then, when you're ready, start to think about the next quilt you want to make as you continue your exciting adventure in the world of quilting.

I have a special wish just for you: may all of your quilts have Happy Endings!

Mimi Dietrich

Introduction

Borders and bindings complement a quilt, much like the matting and frame on a painting. Repeating colors or fabrics from your quilt blocks in the borders unifies and enhances a quilt design. Finish the edges with a crisp, flat binding, and you'll have a quilt you're sure to love.

Before you begin, take the time to read the entire book to see the possibilities for borders and bindings. The basic techniques in the first part of the book give you all the information you need to complete a quilt top.

The project directions will gently guide you through the process of stitching and finishing a table runner or a wall quilt. The patterns are easy, colorful, and fun, and they are geared especially to the beginning quiltmaker. These projects require a minimum number of fabrics, so you need to make only a few decisions as you plan and purchase supplies.

Following the projects, I've listed books that will provide extra help with patchwork, appliqué, and quilting.

As you read, you'll see some symbols alongside the text. Here is what they mean:

Tip boxes include tricks of the trade and handy hints that will make a process or technique a bit easier. Read these right away!

Alert boxes let you know when you really need to be careful. Your guardian angel will alert you so you don't make a common mistake.

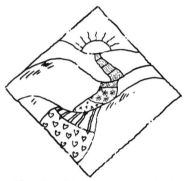

Down the Road boxes contain information that will come in handy on future projects, after you have more quiltmaking experience. You don't need this information right away, though, so feel free to save the Down the Road ideas until you are ready to explore a bit more.

It's exciting to be creative when you choose fabrics and sew them into a quilt. If you are new to quilting, this book will build your confidence as you stitch a small project from start to finish. If you are a more experienced quilter, I hope you have fun with these designs and perhaps try a new border or binding technique.

So, let's begin! Gather your favorite fabrics, tools, and supplies. It's time to start where most quilts end, with borders and bindings.

Border and Binding Terms

Bias Grain: The fabric grain that runs at a 45° angle to the lengthwise and crosswise threads. Fabric has the greatest stretch on the bias grain.

Binding: Fabric strips stitched to the edges of a quilt and folded over to encase the quilt top, batting, and backing.

Blind Stitch: An almost invisible, small stitch used to attach the folded edge of the binding to the back of the quilt. This stitch is the traditional appliqué stitch.

Borders: Strips of fabric that frame the blocks in a quilt. Borders can be whole strips of fabric or pieced patchwork.

Borders with Corner Squares: Borders with a square of fabric in each corner of the quilt.

Double-Fold Binding: Fabric strips folded in half to make a double layer of binding.

Mitered Borders: Borders with a diagonal seam extending from the corner of the pieced section to the corner of the finished quilt.

Multiple-Fabric Borders: Borders made of two or more fabrics.

Pieced Borders: Borders made of fabrics that are pieced to make a design.

Scrappy Patchwork Borders: Borders made of many fabrics from your quilt.

Straight-Cut Borders: Borders applied to opposite edges of your quilt, usually to the sides first, then the top and bottom.

Straight Grain: The straight threads that run the length (lengthwise grain) or width (crosswise grain) of the fabric.

Strip Set: Fabric strips sewn together to make a unit.

Tools and Supplies

You need basic quiltmaking supplies to make your quilt. You probably have most of these supplies in your sewing room now.

Sewing Machine: Make sure your sewing machine is in good working order. If you haven't used it in a long time, treat it to a professional cleaning and oiling. Make sure you have a nice, sharp needle.

Walking Foot or Even-Feed Foot: This sewing machine attachment helps feed the quilt layers into the needle at the same pace. It works in tandem with the feed dogs. The walking foot is particularly helpful for basting the edges of your quilt and applying binding.

Thread: Use all-purpose sewing thread to attach the borders and binding to your quilt.

Needles: Use sharp hand-sewing needles to blindstitch the binding to the back of your quilt.

Pins: Use long, straight pins to pin the borders to your quilt.

Tape Measure: Use a metal or plastic tape measure to accurately measure your quilt.

Masking Tape: Use 1"-wide masking tape to tape mitered borders in place while you sew them.

Sharp Scissors: A good, sharp pair of comfortable shears is necessary for cutting fabric accurately. A small pair of embroidery scissors comes in handy for hand sewing.

Rotary Cutter: This cutting tool has a round, razorlike blade (like a pizza cutter). The blade is extremely sharp and should be used with great care.

Rotary Rulers: There are a number of heavy acrylic rulers in different sizes you can use with the rotary cutter. Use a 6" x 12" or 6" x 24" ruler to cut strips for borders and bindings. Use a 6" square ruler to clean-cut your fabric edges and to square up mitered borders.

Cutting Mat: You must have a surface made for cutting fabric with the rotary cutter. This mat protects your table and helps keep the rotary blade sharp.

Iron: It's very important to have a good steam iron to press seams and to press the fold in the binding.

Low-Loft Batting: Use a thin batting to make it easier to control the quilt layers as you sew the binding on the quilt.

Binding Clips: Use these clips (which resemble hair clips) to hold your quilt binding firmly in place while you hand stitch the back.

Fabric Selection

Selecting fabrics is, of course, a personal matter, but you'll have the most success if you choose border and binding fabrics that balance the color and design in your quilt. It's always safe to use fabrics in the border that you used in your quilt top. Choose one of the darker colors for your borders and binding to frame the quilt and accent the design. Lighter colors tend to make the edges of the quilt fade away.

I had a wonderful time choosing fabrics for the quilt borders in this book. The "Broken Dishes Table Runner" (page 44) border has a delightful design of colorful teacups. The background of this fabric is dark enough to frame the table runner, and the print inspired me to use the Broken Dishes pattern for the blocks. The solid yellow inner border picks up the yellow in the teacup fabric. A striped bias binding adds movement and a spark of color to the edges.

The holiday striped fabric was perfect for the mitered-corner borders in "Holiday Nine Patch" (page 46). The red binding repeats the red in the patchwork blocks.

It was great fun to use the bright colors in "Sparkles" (page 45) to create a pieced border and multicolored binding.

One of my favorite border techniques is to add a narrow ½" to 1" border between the center of the quilt and the outer border. This inner border neatly frames the design and often repeats one of my favorite colors from the quilt. I used this technique in "Button Baskets" (page 42) and "Holiday Nine Patch" (page 46).

If you have finished your quilt, but have not purchased a fabric for your border, it's fun to "audition" fabrics. Take the pieced section of your quilt to your favorite quilt shop and lay it on potential border fabrics to find the one you like best. If you can't find an exact match to the fabrics in your quilt, look for a fabric similar to one of the darker fabrics. A multicolored print that includes several colors in the quilt often makes a successful border.

The print in the border fabric should be proportional to the block size. A very large print may overwhelm your quilt design.

Many quilters design their borders in proportion to the size of the blocks in the quilt: full size, three-quarter size, or half size. All of these combinations give pleasing results, but the border you choose will depend on your quilt and your special tastes. A very wide border may overpower the quilt design, and a very narrow border may give it an unfinished look. Choose a border that complements the design in your quilt.

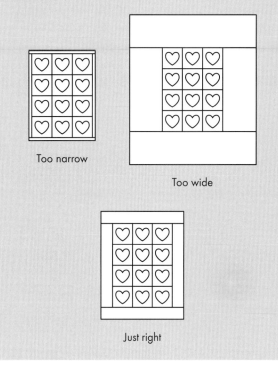

Too narrow

Too wide

Just right

Basic Border Techniques

If you are a beginning quiltmaker, you will no doubt be surprised by the choices you have when it comes to adding borders. On the following pages we'll explore techniques for adding a variety of borders to a quilt top. You might like to start with easy straight-cut borders and tackle the more involved borders a little later. All of the border treatments presented here can be stitched, with success, by careful beginners.

Measuring Your Quilt for Borders

You'll find the measurements for the border strips with each project. It is important, however, to measure your completed quilt top before you cut your borders. If you are making a large quilt or a quilt with many patchwork pieces, the sides of your quilt top may vary in size because everyone pieces a little differently. For this reason, it's always a good idea to cut the borders to match the actual measurements of your quilt top.

Start by measuring the quilt through the center of the patchwork, using a metal or plastic tape measure to ensure accuracy. A center measurement is more accurate because the edges of the quilt may stretch.

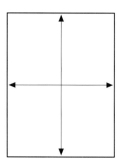

Measuring through the center also helps avoid rippled borders in the finished quilt. Each border technique in this book includes specific directions for measuring your quilt accurately.

This is it—the most important tip in the book! Careful measuring techniques will result in smooth, even borders on your quilt. Always measure your quilt through the center to determine the cut length of the border strips. You will see this tip many times!

Cutting Your Border Strips

Always cut borders on the straight grain of the fabric, never on the bias. Bias edges stretch out of shape easily. Cut your borders with sharp scissors, or use a rotary cutter and rotary ruler.

• If your cut border length is 20" or less, cut two borders at a time across the folded fabric width.

• If your cut border length is between 20" and 40", cut one border at a time across the width of a single layer of fabric.

• If your cut border length is more than 40", cut two borders at a time along the length of a double layer of fabric. (Among the projects in this book, there are no borders longer than 40"—save this information for large quilts in your future.)

When you use a ruler and rotary cutter to cut borders, it is important to cut perfectly straight across your folded fabric. Begin by making a clean-cut edge.

1. Fold the fabric in half lengthwise with the selvages parallel. You may need to raise one cut edge of the fabric in order to align the selvages.

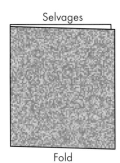

The fabric is even at the left, but the selvages are not parallel.

The selvages are parallel, and the edges are ready to be "clean-cut."

2. Place the fabric on the cutting mat with the fold closest to you and the uneven cut edges to your left. (If you are left-handed, place the uneven edges to your right.) If you prefer, bring the bottom fold up to meet the selvages for a shorter cutting distance.

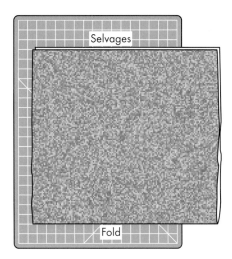

Fabric folded once

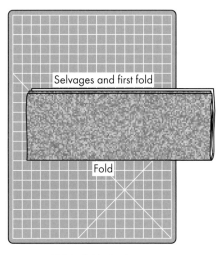

Fabric folded twice

3. Place a 6" square ruler on the bottom fold near the edge to be cut, making sure it is aligned with the fold. Butt a 6" x 24" ruler (or 6" x 12" ruler for double-folded fabric) against the left edge of the square so the edge of the long ruler just covers the uneven cut edges of the fabric. Remove the square and make a clean cut along the edge of the ruler. Roll the rotary cutter away from you, using firm, downward pressure.

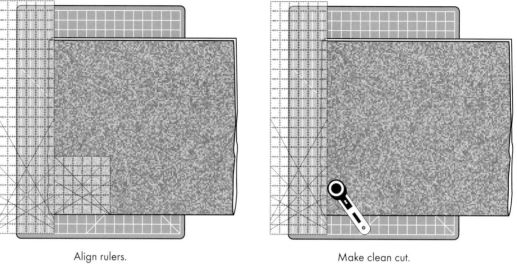

Align rulers.　　　　　Make clean cut.

Right-handed

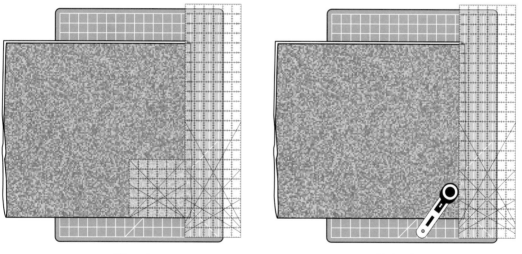

Align rulers.　　　　　Make clean cut.

Left-handed

4. To cut strips, align the clean-cut edge of the fabric with the desired ruler marking and cut. For safety, always cut away from yourself.

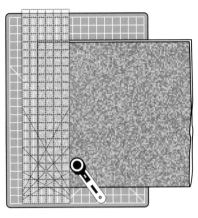

Right-handed

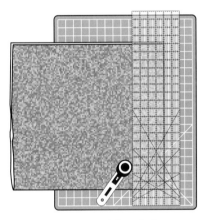

Left-handed

5. Cut the 2 short borders so they measure exactly the same. Repeat with the 2 long borders. (On some quilts, the borders will all be the same length.) Layer one pair of border strips. Cut a straight edge at one end with a rotary cutter and ruler. Repeat with the remaining pair.

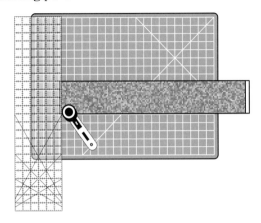

6. Use masking tape to tape the just-cut ends of one pair of borders to your cutting table. Use a measuring tape to determine the correct strip length and mark the point with a pencil. Slip your cutting mat under the marked end and cut the correct length with your rotary cutter. Repeat with the other pair of borders.

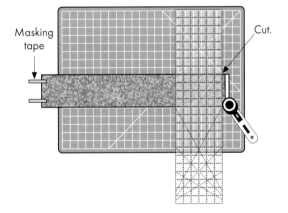

Masking tape

Cut.

Straight-Cut Borders

Straight-cut borders are good to begin with because they are the easiest borders to apply to your quilt. They are sometimes called "over-lapped" borders. "Button Baskets" (page 42) has a pink inner border and a "sewing room" print outer border stitched using this technique.

Border Cutting

2 side borders
2 top and bottom borders

1. Measure the length of the quilt top, from top to bottom, through the center. Cut 2 side border strips to this measurement. Fold each side border in half to find the center and mark with a straight pin. Fold each quilt edge in half and mark with a pin.

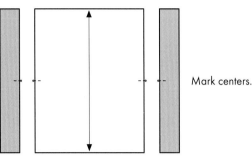

Mark centers.

Measure center of quilt,
top to bottom.

2. With right sides together and raw edges aligned, pin the borders to the quilt top, matching the center pins and the ends. Ease each half of the quilt to fit the borders if necessary. Sew from edge to edge, using a ¼"-wide seam allowance. Press the seam allowances toward the borders.

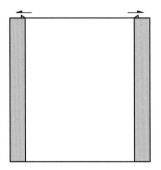

3. Measure the width of the quilt top, from side to side, through the center, including the borders you just attached. Cut the top and bottom border strips to this measurement. Mark the center points of the strips and quilt top with pins.

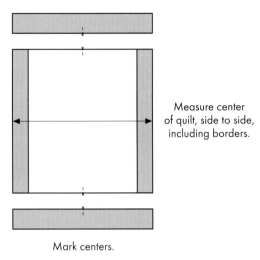

Measure center of quilt, side to side, including borders.

Mark centers.

4. Pin the top and bottom borders to the quilt top as you did the side borders, overlapping the side borders. Sew from edge to edge, using a ¼"-wide seam allowance. Backstitch at the beginning and end of each seam. Press the seam allowances toward the borders. Your borders are finished, ready for binding.

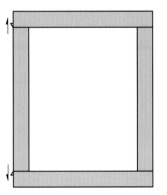

Borders with Corner Squares

Borders with corner squares give a special look to your quilt, adding a color accent at each corner. Look for this technique twice in "Sweet Hearts" (page 43).

Border Cutting
2 side borders
2 top and bottom borders
4 corner squares

Note: On a square quilt, all 4 borders will be the same.

Measure your quilt top through the center to determine the correct border lengths.

Cut the side borders the length of the quilt top, including the seam allowances.

Cut the top and bottom borders the width of the quilt top, including the seam allowances.

Cut 4 corner squares equal in size to the width of the borders. For example, if your border strips are cut 4" wide, cut the corner squares 4" x 4".

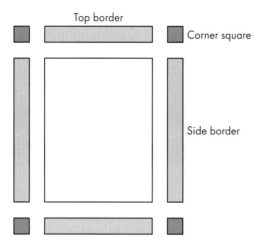

Top border

Corner square

Side border

1. Sew the border strips to opposite sides of the quilt top. Press the seam allowances toward the border strips.

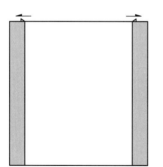

2. Sew a corner square to each end of the top and bottom border strips. Press the seam allowances toward the border strips.

3. Sew the pieced borders to the top and bottom of the quilt top, carefully matching the seams at the corners. Press the seam allowances toward the border strips.

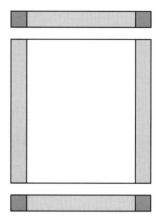

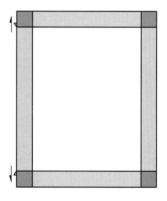

To ensure a good match at the corners, machine baste for a distance of 1" to 2" where the corner squares meet the side borders. Check the borders from the right side. If you think you can improve the match, remove the basting and baste again. When you're satisfied with the match, stitch the borders.

You can use a patchwork block design from your quilt in the corner squares if the borders are the same size as the blocks. Placing a block in each corner unifies and balances the quilt top and the border.

Mitered Borders

Mitered borders have a diagonal seam where two borders meet in the corners, extending from the corner of the pieced or appliquéd section of the quilt to the outer corner. Mitered borders are used in the striped borders on "Holiday Nine Patch" (page 46).

Border Cutting

2 side borders
2 top and bottom borders

Cut the side borders the finished length* of the entire quilt, plus 4" (2" on each end).

Cut the top and bottom borders the finished width of the entire quilt, plus 4" (2" on each end). The Project Information at a Glance will tell you the finished length and width of each project.

Note: On a square quilt, all 4 borders will be the same.

Before adding the mitered border, use a 6" square ruler to make sure that each corner of your quilt is perfectly square. Trim if necessary.

Make corners square.

1. Measure the quilt top from raw edge to raw edge, including the seam allowances. Fold the borders to find the center and mark each with a pin. Also mark half the quilt-top measurement with a pin near each end of each strip.

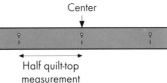

Center

Half quilt-top measurement

2. With right sides together and center pins matching, pin the border strips to the quilt top. Also match the outer pins to the raw edges of the quilt top. Stitch, leaving ¼" of the quilt top unstitched at the beginning and end of each seam; backstitch. Press the seams toward the borders.

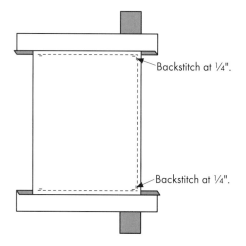

Backstitch at ¼".

Backstitch at ¼".

3. With the quilt right side up, lay the first corner to be mitered on your ironing board. Pin the quilt to the ironing board to keep it from pulling and the corner from slipping. Position the quilt and borders as shown, with the vertical border overlapping the horizontal border.

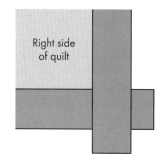

Right side of quilt

4. Fold the vertical border under at a 45° angle. Work with the fold until the borders meet evenly.

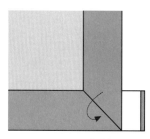

Fold.

5. Place pins through all layers at the fold. Place your 6" square ruler over the corner to check that the corner is flat and square. Adjust the border for a perfect miter if necessary. When everything is straight and square, remove the pins and press the fold with a steam iron.

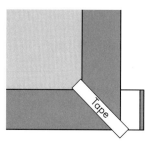

6. Carefully center a piece of 1"-wide masking tape over the mitered fold.

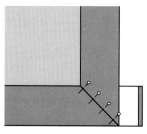

Tape

7. Unpin the quilt from the ironing board and turn down the vertical border, folding the center section of the quilt diagonally. Draw a light pencil line in the pressed crease. Carefully align the long edges of the border strips.

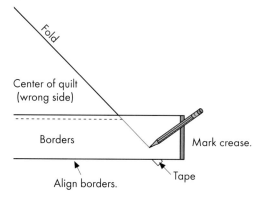

Fold

Center of quilt (wrong side)

Borders

Mark crease.

Align borders.

Tape

8. Sew on the pencil line, being careful not to sew through the tape. Remove the tape. You've made your first miter!

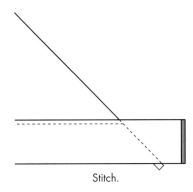

Stitch.

9. Check once more to make sure the borders lie flat; then trim the excess fabric, leaving a ¼"-wide seam allowance. Press the seam open for a perfect mitered corner.

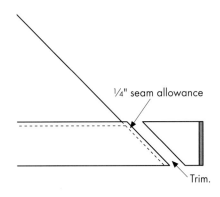

¼" seam allowance

Trim.

10. Repeat these steps for the remaining 3 mitered corners.

If you wish, you can use appliqué stitches to complete the mitered corner. Instead of using masking tape, pin the miter carefully. Appliqué the fold; then trim the excess fabric.

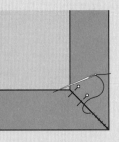

Appliqué the fold.

Hooray for stripes! Use a striped fabric for wonderful mitered borders. Cut the stripes following the printed lines, adding ¼"-wide seam allowances and making sure that the same design is centered in each strip.

Multiple-Fabric Borders

Multiple-fabric borders consist of two or more border strips on each edge of a quilt. Although they look complex, these borders are in fact easy to make if you sew them using one of four techniques.

Multiple-fabric borders often graduate in size, becoming wider toward the edge of the quilt. You'll find these borders in "Button Baskets" (page 42), "Broken Dishes Table Runner" (page 44), and "Holiday Nine Patch" (page 46). Repeat a color or fabric from the quilt in the borders to accent the design.

Border Cutting

    2 inner side borders
    2 outer side borders
    2 inner top and bottom borders
    2 outer top and bottom borders

 Measure your quilt top through the center to determine the correct border lengths.

Multiple-Fabric Border I

To use the straight-cut border technique (page 14) for a multiple-fabric border, sew the borders to the quilt top one round at a time. Add all four strips of the same fabric before adding strips of the next fabric, pressing each seam allowance toward the new border.

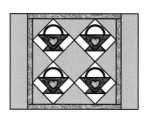

Multiple-Fabric Border II

To use the borders-with-corner-squares method (page 15) for a multiple-fabric border, complete the inner border with corner squares, followed by the outer border with corner squares, just as you would two separate borders.

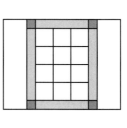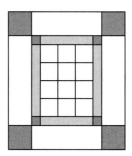

Multiple-Fabric Border III

You can combine pieced borders and corner squares to make yet another variation on a multiple-fabric border. The "Broken Dishes Table Runner" (page 44) features this border.

1. Measure the quilt top and cut the border strips and corner squares, following the directions for "Borders with Corner Squares" (page 15).
2. Sew the border strips together to make 4 complete borders, one for each side.
3. Treat these multiple-fabric borders as single borders and add them to the quilt top along with the corner squares.

Multiple-Fabric Border IV

Multiple-fabric borders with mitered corners are impressive—and surprisingly easy to make. "Holiday Nine Patch" (page 46) has this border.

1. Measure the quilt top and cut the border strips, following the directions for "Mitered Borders" (page 17).
2. Sew the border strips together to make 4 complete borders, one border for each side.
3. Treat these multiple-fabric borders as single borders and add them to the quilt top, following the directions for "Mitered Borders." Carefully match the border seams as you miter the corners.

Pieced Borders

You have many wonderful design options when it comes to pieced borders. I used a strip-pieced checkerboard border to frame the House blocks in "Home Sweet Home" (page 41). For the steps that follow, we'll use this border as an example. It's fun, easy, and fast to sew!

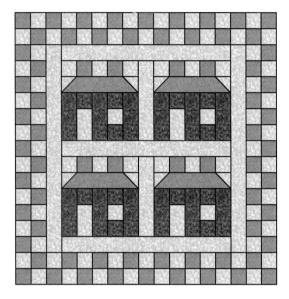

 Be careful as you sew a pieced border. If your seam allowance isn't a precise ¼", your pieced border will probably shrink or grow, requiring you to rip and resew. Check your seam allowance guide before you begin stitching your border. Slight variations in seam allowances really add up in a pieced border.

Border Cutting

4 strips of light fabric, each 2½" x 40"
4 strips of dark fabric, each 2½" x 40"

 Measure your quilt top through the center to determine the accurate size of your quilt.

1. Sew a light strip to a dark strip. Make 4 strip sets. Sew the strips with a small stitch length (20 stitches per inch) on your machine. The small stitches will hold the little pieces together securely when you crosscut the strip sets.

   Press the seam allowances toward the dark strip on all of the strip sets. When you cut and sew the segments together, the seam allowances will lock and match perfectly. Use a ruler and rotary cutter to clean-cut the edges of each strip set. Crosscut the strip sets into 16 segments, each 2½" wide.

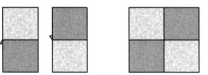

2. Sew 13 segments together, reversing the light and dark squares each time you sew. Make 2 border units.

Make 2.

3. Sew the border units to opposite sides of the quilt top. Make sure you place light squares at the edges of the quilt top. Press the seam allowances toward the sashing strips.

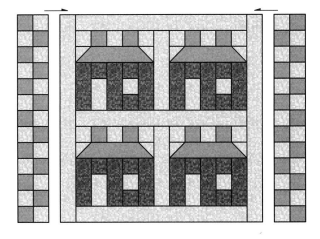

 If your pieced borders do not match the edges of the quilt, it's OK to "fudge." If the border strip is too long, go back and sew over a few seams to make it a little shorter. If the border is too short, take out a few seams and stitch slightly smaller seam allowances.

4. Sew 17 units together, reversing the light and dark squares each time you sew. Make 2 border units. Sew these border units to the top and bottom of the quilt top. Make sure you place dark squares in the outer corners of the quilt. Press the seam allowances toward the sashing strips.

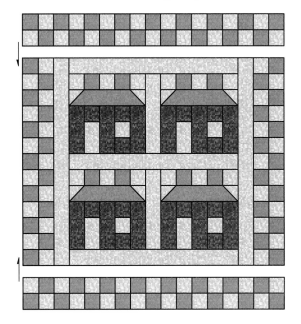

If you use this checkerboard border on another quilt, the quilt-top measurements, not including the seam allowances, must be divisible by 2. You may need to cut a different number of strips and segments.

Scrappy Patchwork Borders

To create a unique border with a scrappy look, repeat some or all of the fabrics from your quilt in a pieced border. For the following steps, we'll use the scrappy pieced border on "Sparkles" (page 45) as an example.

Border Cutting

Cut a strip of each fabric used in the quilt.

For your strips, cut a variety of widths, or use a consistent width that relates to the size of the blocks or pieces in your quilt. The "Sparkles" border is made with strips cut 2" wide, resulting in a 1½"-wide border (¼ the size of the 6" Pinwheel blocks). The quilt-top measurements through the center, not including the seam allowances, must be divisible by 1½ for this border to fit.

If you want to make a pieced border for a quilt top that is not divisible by 1½, it's easiest to vary the width of the strips and add or subtract pieces as needed.

1. Sew the fabric strips together to make a strip set. Use a ruler and rotary cutter to clean-cut the edges of the strip set. Cross-cut the strip set into segments 2" wide. For a different-width border, cut segments the finished width plus ½" for seam allowances.

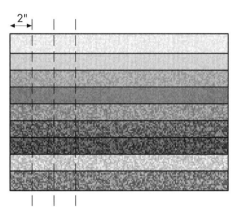

Measure your quilt top through the center to determine the correct border lengths.

2. Sew the segments together to create borders that are the correct length for the sides of your quilt top. Add or subtract patchwork pieces if necessary.

3. Sew the strips to opposite sides of the quilt top. Press the seam allowances toward the sashing strips.

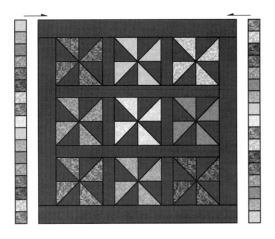

4. Sew the segments together to create borders that are the correct length for the top and bottom edges of your quilt top. Add or subtract pieces if necessary.

5. Sew the border strips to the top and bottom edges. Press the seam allowances toward the sashing strips.

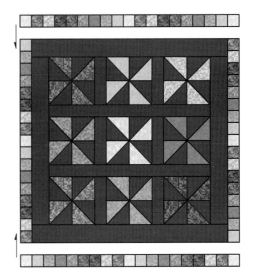

Basic Binding Techniques

Binding made from one of the fabrics in your quilt is the perfect way to finish the edges. Quilters usually choose a dark or bright fabric from their quilt to frame the design. The projects in this book include binding fabric in the materials list.

The double-fold method is my favorite way to apply binding. This technique places two layers of fabric over the edge of the quilt, creating a neat, durable binding.

Always prewash your fabric when you are making binding. This step prevents the binding from shrinking and puckering after you apply it to your quilt.

Preparing and Measuring Your Quilt

After you finish quilting your quilt, it's important to take a little time to prepare your quilt for the binding. It's especially important to baste the layers together at the edges. It is much easier to sew the binding to "one quilt" rather than "three layers."

1. Remove any basting stitches or pins used in the quilting process.

2. Lay your quilt on a flat surface with the quilt top up. Carefully smooth the quilt top, batting, and backing. Pin the layers securely around the edges, placing the pins about 3" apart through all layers.

3. Using a walking foot or even-feed foot on your sewing machine, baste the edges ⅛" from the cut edge of the quilt top. If you wish, baste the edges by hand.

4. Use a ruler and rotary cutter to trim the batting, backing, and any excess threads even with the quilt top.

5. Use your 6" square ruler to make sure that the corners are square. Trim if necessary.

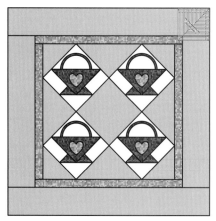

Make corners square.

Check the opposite sides of your quilt to make sure they are even. You can adjust the length of the edges by tightening or loosening the basting stitches.

6. To determine the length of binding required for your project, measure around the perimeter of your quilt and add 10". Remember this number! You will need a strip of binding at least this long to finish your quilt.

Straight-Grain Binding

Straight-grain binding is cut along the straight grain of the fabric, either the lengthwise or the crosswise grain. You can use straight-grain binding on any quilt, table runner, or wall hanging that has straight edges and square corners. The projects in this book, with the exception of the "Broken Dishes Table Runner" (page 44), are made with straight-grain binding. The project directions tell you how many binding strips to cut.

When you use a ruler and rotary cutter to cut binding, it's important to cut perfectly straight across your folded fabric. Turn to "Cutting Your Border Strips," steps 1–4, on pages 10–13 to cut your binding strips. Cut the strips 2" wide.

Thanks to Carol Doak and *Your First Quilt Book (or it should be!)*, we have a chart that tells us approximately how much 2"-wide crosswise binding you can cut from 44"-wide yardage.

2"-wide Straight-Grain Binding

¼ yd.	4 strips x 44" = 176"
⅓ yd.	6 strips x 44" = 264"
½ yd.	9 strips x 44" = 396"

Joining Binding Strips

Diagonal seams distribute the bulk of the seams as they go over and around the edges of the quilt. The following technique for joining strips is one of my Top Ten quilting tips.

1. Cross 2 strip ends at right angles, right sides together. Lay them on a flat surface and pin securely.

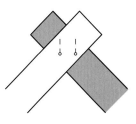

2. Imagine the strips as a large letter "A." Draw a line across the crossed pieces to "cross the A"; then sew along the line. Your seam will be exact and your strip continuous.

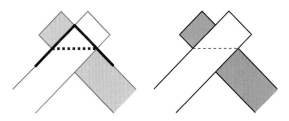

3. Trim the excess fabric, leaving a ¼"-wide seam allowance.

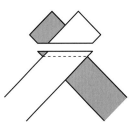

4. Press the seam open to distribute the bulk.

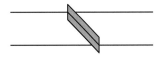

5. Continue adding strips until you have enough binding to go around your quilt, plus 10".

Folding the Binding

Fold the binding strip in half lengthwise, wrong sides together, and press with a hot steam iron, using an up-and-down (not back-and-forth) motion.

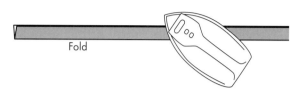

Fold

 As you press the binding, let the bottom layer extend slightly. When you sew the binding to your quilt, you will be able to see both layers, and you will be in control if one shifts or unfolds.

Let bottom layer extend slightly.

Sewing Binding to Your Quilt

If you plan to add a hanging sleeve, do so now. See "Adding a Sleeve" on page 35.

Before you sew the binding to your quilt, take a moment to think about the starting point. Do not start attaching the binding in a corner. It's much easier to fold a miter at the corner than to sew it there! Also avoid the middle of the sides of the quilt. If you start there, each time you fold the quilt in half, it will weaken this spot. It's best to start approximately 6" from one of the corners.

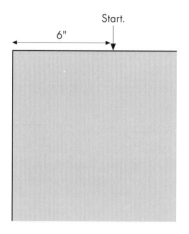

Start.

6"

1. Match the cut edges of the binding strip to the cut edges of the quilt.

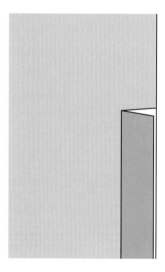

2. To get a good start, pin the first 10" of binding. As you gain experience, you won't find it necessary to pin, even at the beginning.

3. Using a walking foot or even-feed foot, start sewing 4" from the beginning of the binding. Use a ¼"-wide seam allowance and a stitch length of 10 stitches per inch.

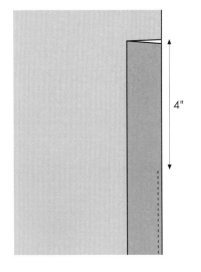

Sewing Hints

• Do not pin the binding to the entire quilt before sewing. As you sew, the binding may "bubble up" between the pins and cause little tucks. It's also very uncomfortable to sew with all those pins sticking you.

• As you sew, concentrate on the three inches of binding directly in front of the needle. Lay these three inches in position and sew; then go on to the next three inches. Before long, these three inches will add up to the entire quilt!

• Be careful not to stretch the binding as you sew. Keep the long piece of binding in your lap, rather than letting it fall to the floor.

• Use a long straight pin to control the layers in front of the presser foot and needle as you sew. This technique will prevent you from sticking your finger under the needle—the straight pin fits under there much better.

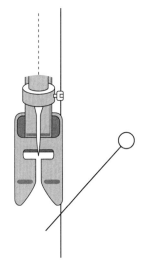

Many quilters measure the ¼" seam allowance by matching the fabric with the edge of the presser foot. When you use a walking foot, this seam may be too wide. You may be able to adjust the needle position on your machine by moving the needle to the right. You can also place a piece of masking tape on your machine to mark the ¼" seam allowance. Test the seam allowance on a scrap of fabric before sewing the binding to your quilt.

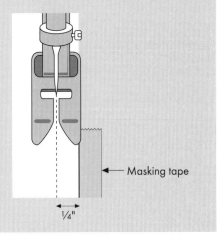

Mitering the Corners

Mitered corners give a professional finish to your binding. If mitered corners make you nervous, relax—there are only four corners, and you will be an expert by the third one.

1. Continue sewing the binding to the first edge of the quilt top. Stop stitching ¼" from the corner and backstitch.

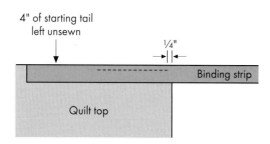

4" of starting tail left unsewn

¼"

Binding strip

Quilt top

Straight pins help you mark the exact place to stop stitching. Turn your quilt to the wrong side and stick a pin into the corner so that it is ¼" from each of the edges. Push it straight through all layers (quilt plus binding). The place where the pin comes out on top marks the place where you will stop stitching. Take another pin and insert it from the front into this spot. Use the second pin to hold the binding and quilt together. "Where the pin goes in" marks the place to stop stitching.

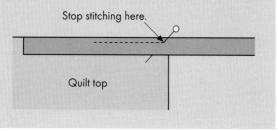

Stop stitching here.

Quilt top

2. Fold the binding diagonally as shown, so that it extends straight up from the second edge of the quilt. This fold creates the miter.

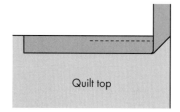

Quilt top

3. Fold the binding down, even with the second edge of the quilt. The fold should be even with the first (upper) edge. Use 2 pins to hold the fold in place.

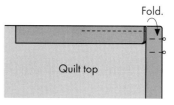

Fold.

Quilt top

4. Start sewing the binding ¼" from the fold, making sure to backstitch. This line of stitching continues the line of stitching from the first edge.

Quilt top

5. Repeat steps 1–4 for the remaining corners.

If it looks as though a binding seam will occur near the miter fold, you can choose to ignore it and live with a little bulk. If you prefer, remove the quilt from the machine and reseam the binding so the seam falls before the miter.

Connecting the Ends

You have several options when it comes time to connect the starting and finishing ends of the binding. The straight-and-easy connection is the easiest. The diagonal connection looks just like one of the binding seams.

Straight-and-Easy Connection

1. As you approach the beginning of the binding, stop approximately 4" from the start of the binding strip and remove the quilt from the machine.
2. Overlap the end of the binding ½" from the start of the binding and trim the excess.

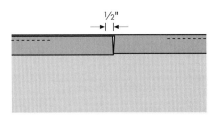

3. Open the folds of the 2 strips and sew the ends together with a ¼"-wide seam allowance. Press the seam allowance open.

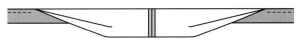

4. Refold the seamed section of the strip, return it to the edge of the quilt, and finish sewing the binding.

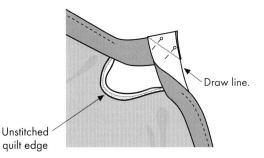

Diagonal Connection

1. As you approach the beginning, stop approximately 4" from the start of the binding strip and remove the quilt from the sewing machine.
2. Overlap the end of the binding strip 2" from the start of the binding strip and trim the excess.

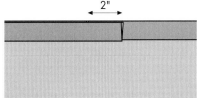

3. Open the folds of the 2 strips and overlap them at right angles with right sides together; pin. Draw a diagonal line as shown.

Draw line.

Unstitched quilt edge

4. Sew the ends together on the line. Trim the excess fabric to ¼". Press the seam allowance open.

Trim.

5. Refold the seamed section of the strip, return it to the edge of the quilt, and finish sewing the binding.

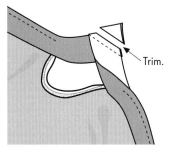

Bias-Grain Binding

Binding that is cut on the bias grain of the fabric has more stretch than binding cut on the straight grain. Bias-grain binding is necessary if the edges of your quilt are curved or if the corners are rounded.

You can also use bias binding on a quilt with straight edges. Stripes and plaids look great made into bias binding because the design lines fall on the diagonal, creating a wrap-around effect at the edges. The "Broken Dishes Table Runner" (page 44) features a bias binding made of striped fabric.

1. To cut bias strips, fold a fabric square in half diagonally and press. Fold the square diagonally a second time.

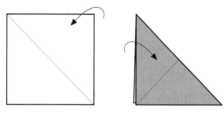

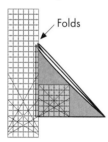

Two folds

2. Make a clean cut to remove the 2 folds. Cut 2"-wide strips.

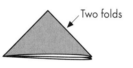

Folds

Remove both folds.   Cut bias strips.

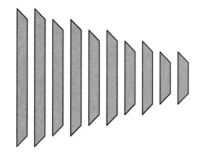

3. Join the strips as shown with a ¼"-wide seam allowance.

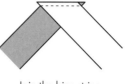

Join the bias strips.

The following chart tells you approximately how much 2"-wide bias-grain binding can be cut from a particular square.

Size of Square	Length of 2"-wide Bias Binding
20"	150"
22"	200"
24"	250"
26"	290"

On bias strips, the beginning of the binding will look different because the end is on an angle.

Attach this binding as you would straight-grain binding (page 27). Use a diagonal connection (page 31) to join the ends. In step 2, trim the angled ends straight across so they overlap by 2".

Finishing the Back of Your Quilt

Now you are ready to fold the binding to the back of your quilt and stitch it in place.

Folding the Binding over the Edge

1. On the quilt front, place your finger under a corner fold and push the fabric toward the point.

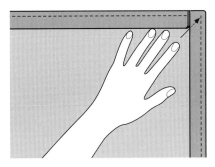

2. Fold the binding over the edge and toward the back. On the front, the fabric automatically folds into the miter.

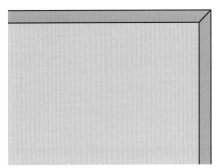

3. On the back, fold the binding flat over one edge of the quilt. At the corner, the binding will form a diagonal fold.

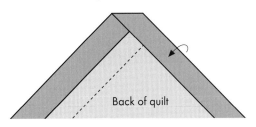

Back of quilt

4. As you turn under the second edge, the diagonal fold creates a miter on the back of the quilt.

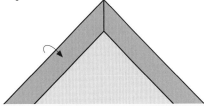

As you fold the binding to the back, work from the back of the quilt and fold the right edge first, followed by the left. Look closely; this technique distributes the thickness of the fabric evenly at the point.

Sewing the Binding to the Back

The blind stitch, or appliqué stitch, allows you to sew the binding to the back of the quilt with tiny stitches that barely show.

1. Pin the binding to the back of the quilt so the folded edge just covers the machine stitching.

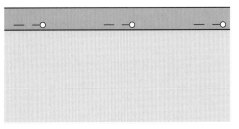

Use thread to match the color of the binding and a sharp hand-sewing needle. Thread the needle with a single strand of sewing thread approximately 18" long and knot the long end.

2. Insert the threaded needle under the edge of the binding, close to the fold.

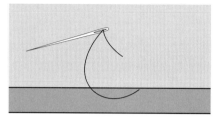

3. Insert the needle directly across from where it went into the binding, into the batting and backing only. Place your other hand under the edge of the quilt to make sure the needle does not go through the top. (You don't want to see the stitches on the front of the quilt.)

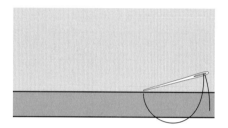

4. Slide the needle under the backing and batting about ⅛", then bring it up through the backing into the folded edge of the binding. Repeat until you near the corner.

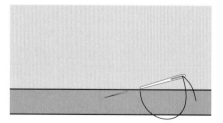

5. When you get to the corner miters, you will feel great if you take a moment to stitch the miters closed. Starting on the back, take 3 stitches on the miter.

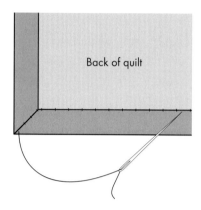

6. Stick the needle through to the front of the quilt and take 3 stitches in the front seam. Stick the needle through to the back of the quilt and continue sewing the binding to the back.

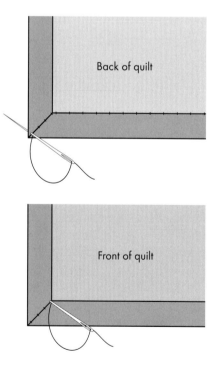

7. To end the thread, take 2 or 3 stitches in the same place along the edge of the binding. Slide the needle through the binding to hide the end of the thread and cut.

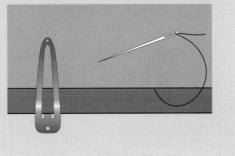

 Instead of pins, I use four binding clips, moving them as I go, to hold the binding in place as I stitch it to the back of the quilt.

Adding a Sleeve

If you are planning to hang your quilt on a wall (or in a quilt show), sew a sleeve to the back as you apply the binding.

1. Cut a strip of fabric as long as the width of your quilt and 8½" wide. This strip will make a 4"-wide sleeve.

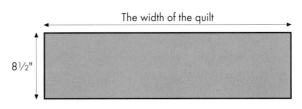

The width of the quilt

8½"

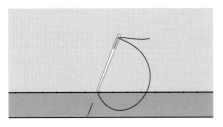 To create a deeper sleeve, double the desired finished width and add ½" for seam allowances. If, for example, you wish to add a 6"-wide sleeve, cut the sleeve 12½" wide.

2. Turn under ¼" twice at each end of the strip and stitch a narrow hem.

3. Fold the sleeve, wrong sides together, and pin the raw edges to the top of the quilt before you attach the binding. Machine baste ⅛" from the top edge.

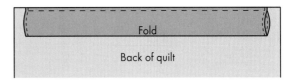

Fold

Back of quilt

4. Sew the binding to the quilt.
5. Blindstitch the folded edge of the sleeve to the back of the quilt. Be very careful not to stitch through to the front of the quilt.

Finishing Your Quilt with Backing
(an alternative to binding)

Some quilts appear to have binding along the edges but are actually finished by turning the backing fabric to the front, over the batting and quilt top. If you choose to finish your quilt this way, be sure that your backing fabric coordinates with the block and border fabrics.

Finishing your quilt with backing requires that you cut the backing larger than the quilt top. Often, the backing is already longer and wider than the quilt top. This technique is an economical way to use that extra fabric.

Think about the use of your quilt when you are considering this technique. It's great for wall quilts, but probably not durable enough for baby quilts or other quilts that will be washed often.

Preparing Your Quilt

1. After quilting your project, use scissors to trim the batting even with the edge of the quilt top. Be careful not to cut the backing.

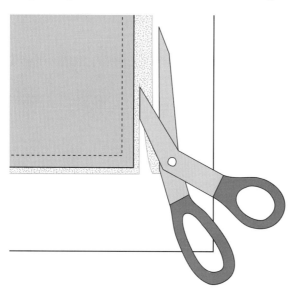

2. Lay the quilt on a flat surface and baste around the edges, ¼" from the edge of the quilt top. Be sure to stitch through the quilt top, batting, and backing. This step will keep the layers from shifting as you finish the edges.

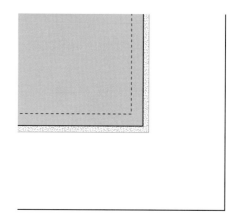

3. For ½"-wide "binding," you will need 1" of backing fabric extending beyond the edge of the quilt top. Use a rotary ruler to measure 1" of extra fabric around the edges of the quilt top. Trim the backing carefully.

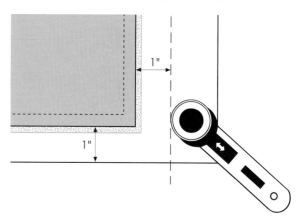

Straight Edges

1. Fold the 1" of backing fabric in half, wrong sides together, so that the cut edge of the backing just meets the cut edge of the quilt top.

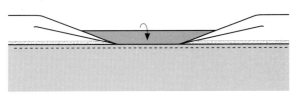

2. Fold the backing again along the edge of the quilt top to form the finished edge. This fold encases the batting and covers ½" of the quilt top. Pin along the first fold to hold the "binding" in place.

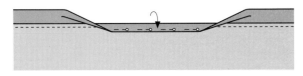

Overlapped Corners

You can finish the corners with either of two methods. The easiest method is to fold the first side, extending the folds to the ends. Then fold the second side, overlapping the first side at the corners.

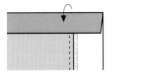

This method is easy. It can be bulky, however, and threads sometimes sneak out of the corner folds. Fold the corners carefully and sew them closed.

Mitered Corners

Mitering the corners is easier than you think, and this technique produces a neat, crisp edge.

1. Fold the corner of the backing over the corner point of the quilt top so that the fold touches the point.

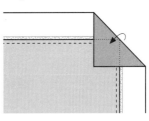

2. Fold the 1" of backing fabric in half, wrong sides together, so that the cut edge of the backing just meets the cut edge of the quilt top.

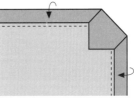

3. Fold the backing once more to create the "binding" and a miter at the corner. Trim the small square that extends onto the quilt. Pin the folds securely.

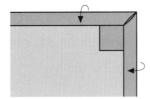 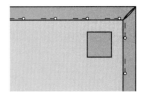

Finishing

You can finish the "binding" by hand or by machine.

Finishing by Hand

1. Use an 18" length of thread that matches the backing fabric. Blindstitch the folded edge to the front of the quilt (page 34). The stitches should not go through to the back of the quilt. At each mitered corner, close the miter with 4 or 5 blind stitches; then continue to sew the next side of the quilt.

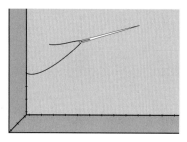

2. After you stitch the binding, quilt a row of stitches next to the binding, sewing through all 3 layers of your quilt. This quilting will secure the edges and give the illusion of binding on the back of the quilt. Don't forget to remove your basting stitches.

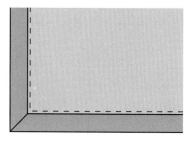

Finishing by Machine

To finish by machine, simply sew around the edges of the quilt on the fold. This stitching sews through all layers of the quilt, so it is not necessary to add the last row of quilting stitches. Close the corner miters with a few small blind stitches.

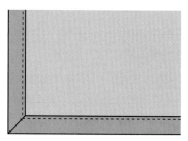

Signing Your Quilt

You did it! You made a fabulous quilt. Make a label for the back of your quilt and sign your name and date. I encourage you to also include special information about the quilt; those who admire your quilt in years to come will enjoy and appreciate its story.

Projects

These projects were designed just for you, the beginner, to give you the chance to try the border techniques you learned in the first chapter. Among these six projects, you'll find a variety of patchwork and appliqué designs. To help you make your quilt, the following information is provided with each project:

• The colors and amounts of fabric you'll need

• Cutting directions for the borders and setting pieces

• Cutting directions for the patchwork and appliqué pieces

• Step-by-step instructions for making the blocks

• Step-by-step instructions for assembling the project

Small, one-sided pressing arrows let you know which way to press the seam allowances.

The cutting instructions for the setting and block pieces are for rotary cutting. If you prefer to cut the block pieces by hand, you'll find templates with each project.

Gallery

Home Sweet Home *by Mimi Dietrich, 1998, Baltimore, Maryland, 34½" x 34½"; quilted by Linda Newsom. A pieced checkerboard border adds a country look to this Little House quilt.*

Button Baskets *by Mimi Dietrich, 1998, Baltimore, Maryland, 26½" x 26½"; quilted by Linda Newsom. Straight-cut borders make an easy frame for baskets filled with buttons.*

Sweet Hearts *by Mimi Dietrich, 1998, Baltimore, Maryland,*
23½" x 23½"; quilted by Mimi Dietrich. Borders with corner squares
frame a charming appliqué design in this pretty little quilt.

Broken Dishes Table Runner
*by Mimi Dietrich, 1998,
Baltimore, Maryland,
19½" x 39½"; quilted by Linda
Newson. Multiple-fabric borders
with corner squares surround a
lively Broken Dishes patchwork
design. The teacup fabric
suggested the block pattern.*

Sparkles *by Mimi Dietrich, 1998, Baltimore, Maryland, 37" x 37";*
quilted by Linda Newsom. A scrappy border and patchwork binding
combine with metallic thread in this luminous Pinwheel quilt.

Holiday Nine Patch *by Mimi Dietrich, 1998, Baltimore, Maryland, 30" x 30"; quilted by Linda Newsom. A striped fabric is ideally suited to mitered borders.*

Button Baskets

Here's your opportunity to practice both appliqué and patchwork on a quilt with simple, straight-cut borders. Most quilt borders are stitched using this basic technique.

The Basket blocks are set on point, and the setting triangles between the blocks have bias edges. To avoid stretching, be sure to pin these seams carefully before you sew.

Color photo on page 42.

Project Information at a Glance

Finished Quilt Size:	26½" x 26½"
Name of Block:	Button Baskets
Finished Block Size:	6" x 6"
Number of Blocks to Make:	4
Setting:	On point
Border Treatment:	Straight-Cut Borders
Finished Inner Border Width:	1"
Finished Outer Border Width:	3½"
Binding:	Straight-Grain

Materials: 44"-wide fabric

1½ yds. "sewing room" print for setting pieces, outer border, and backing
½ yd. blue print for baskets and binding
⅜ yd. pink print for hearts and inner border
¼ yd. tan fabric for basket background
12 pink buttons for baskets
31" x 31" square of low-loft batting

Letters identify templates and rotary-cut pieces.

Cutting Setting Pieces and Borders

From the "sewing room" print, cut:
  1 piece, 31" x 31", for backing
  1 square, 6½" x 6½", for setting square
  1 square, 9¾" x 9¾"; cut the square twice
    diagonally for a total of 4 side setting
    triangles

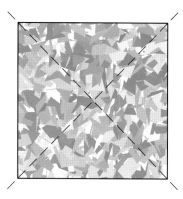

2 squares, each 5¼" x 5¼"; cut each square
  once diagonally for a total of 4 corner setting triangles

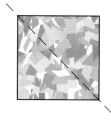

2 strips, each 4" x 19½", for outer borders
2 strips, each 4" x 26½", for outer borders

From the blue print, cut:
  3 strips, each 2" x 40", for binding

From the pink print, cut:
  2 strips, each 1½" x 17½", for inner borders
  2 strips, each 1½" x 19½", for inner borders

Cutting Block Pieces

Note: If you prefer to use templates to cut the block pieces, turn to page 76.

Fabric	No. of Pieces	1st Cut	2nd Cut	Yield	Placement
Tan	8	2" x 3½"		8	A
	2	3⅞" x 3⅞"	◹	4	D
	2	5⅜" x 5⅜"	◹	4	E
Blue	2	5⅜" x 5⅜"	◹	4	C
	4	2⅜" x 2⅜"	◹	8	B

◹ *Cut the squares once diagonally.*

Cutting Appliqué Pieces

Fabric	No. of Pieces	Size to Cut	Placement
Blue	4	¾" x 7½"*	F (basket handle)
Pink	4		G (heart)

*Cut these strips on the bias.

Block Assembly

The following directions are for making one Basket block. You can make one block at a time or all four blocks in assembly-line fashion.

Before you start to sew, arrange the patchwork pieces for each block as shown. Set aside the blue basket handle (F).

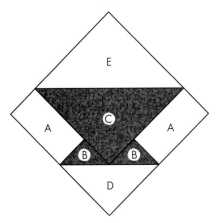

1. Sew a blue triangle (B) to a tan rectangle (A) to make the left side of the basket.

2. Sew a blue triangle (B) to a tan rectangle (A) to make the right side of the basket.

3. Sew the units from steps 1 and 2 to the large blue triangle (C).

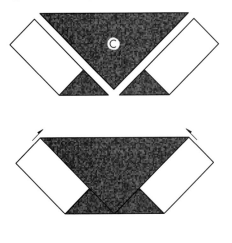

4. Sew the tan triangle (D) to the bottom of the basket.

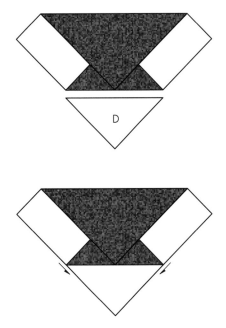

5. Trace the basket handle placement line onto the tan triangle (E).

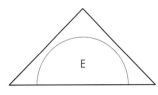

6. Fold the blue basket handle (F) in half lengthwise, wrong sides together. Press with a steam iron or baste close to the raw edges through both layers.

7. Place the raw edges of the handle just inside the placement line. Using small running stitches, sew the strip to the background almost through the center of the strip, slightly closer to the raw edges than to the fold.

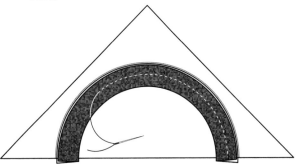

8. Roll the folded edge over the raw edges. Appliqué the fold to the background fabric to create a smooth handle.

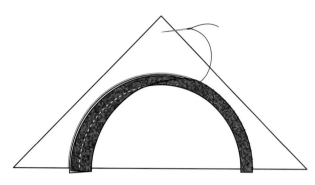

Cut a paper "window" for perfect placement of the heart. Here's how:
1. Trace the blue triangle basket piece (C) and the heart (G) onto plain white paper.
2. Cut out the triangle; then carefully cut out the heart to create a window.
3. Place the paper window over the blue fabric triangle. Drop the prepared heart appliqué through the window for perfect placement.

9. Sew the appliquéd triangle to the top of the basket.

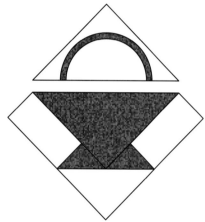

10. Appliqué the pink heart (G) to the basket to finish the block.

Quilt Assembly

1. Arrange the Basket blocks and setting pieces as shown. Sew the blocks and triangles together in diagonal rows. Press the seam allowances toward the setting triangles and center setting square.

2. Sew the rows together, adding corner triangles 3 and 4 last.
3. Sew the 1½" x 17½" pink border strips to opposite sides of the quilt top. Sew the 1½" x 19½" pink border strips to the top and bottom edges of the quilt top.

4. Sew the 4" x 19½" "sewing room" border strips to opposite sides of the quilt top. Sew the 4" x 26½" "sewing room" border strips to the top and bottom edges of the quilt top.

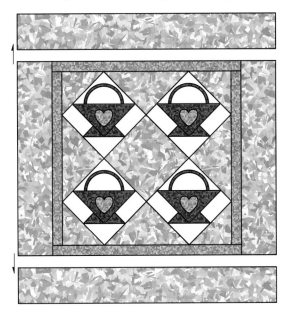

Finishing

1. Layer the quilt top with batting and backing; baste.
2. Outline quilt around the appliqué pieces, patchwork pieces, setting square, setting triangles, and borders. See the quilting suggestion below for the border, setting square, and setting triangles.

3. Bind the edges with the 2"-wide blue strips.
4. Sew 3 buttons inside each handle.
5. Add a label to the back of your finished quilt.

Sweet Hearts

The corner squares in the borders of this little quilt repeat the pretty pink fabrics in the appliquéd hearts. The secret to sewing these borders lies in pressing the corner-square seams so they match perfectly.

Color photo on page 43.

Project Information at a Glance	
Finished Quilt Size:	23½" x 23½"
Name of Block:	Sweet Hearts
Finished Block Size:	8" x 8"
Number of Blocks to Make:	1
Setting:	On Point
Border Treatment:	Borders with Corner Squares
Finished Inner Border Width:	2"
Finished Outer Border Width:	3"
Binding:	Straight-Grain

Materials: 44"-wide fabric

1 yd. off-white print for block background, setting triangles, and backing

¼ yd. pink print for corner squares and appliquéd hearts

⅜ yd. green print for inner borders, binding, and appliquéd leaves

⅜ yd. blue print for outer borders and appliquéd ribbon

28" x 28" square of low-loft batting

Letters identify templates.

Cutting Setting Pieces and Borders

From the off-white print, cut:
  1 piece, 28" x 28", for backing
  1 square, 8½" x 8½", for appliqué background
  2 squares, each 9⅜" x 9⅜"; cut each square
    once diagonally for a total of 4 corner
    setting triangles

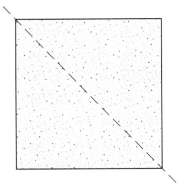

From the pink print, cut:
  4 squares, each 2½" x 2½", for inner border
    corner squares
  4 squares, each 3½" x 3½", for outer border
    corner squares

From the green print, cut:
  4 strips, each 2½" x 8½", for inner borders
  3 strips, each 2" x 40", for binding

From the blue print, cut:
  4 strips, each 3½" x 17½", for outer borders

Cutting Appliqué Pieces

Use the full-size appliqué pattern on page 75 and your favorite method to cut and prepare the following pieces.

Fabric	Number to Cut	Piece
Blue	1 ribbon (left)	1
	1 ribbon (right)	2
Pink	4 hearts	3
Green	2 leaves	4

Block Assembly

1. Center the 8½" background square over the full-size appliqué pattern and trace the appliqué design.
2. Appliqué the ribbons, letting the tops of the ribbons lie flat under the placement lines for the center heart.

3. Appliqué the hearts.

4. Appliqué the leaves.

Quilt Assembly

1. Sew the 2½" x 8½" green border strips to opposite sides of the center block.

2. Sew a 2½" pink corner square to each end of the 2 remaining border strips.

3. Sew the pieced borders to the top and bottom to complete the border.

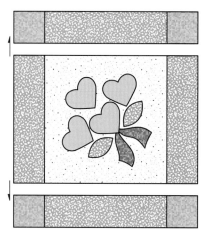

4. Sew an off-white triangle to opposite sides of the quilt.

5. Add an off-white triangle to each of the remaining sides.

Carefully match the seam allowances where each corner square meets the border. Because the seam allowances are pressed in opposite directions, they will lock and match perfectly.

6. Sew the 3½" x 17½" blue border strips to opposite sides of the quilt.

7. Sew a 3½" pink corner square to each end of the 2 remaining border strips.

8. Sew the pieced borders to the top and bottom to complete the quilt top.

Finishing

1. Layer the quilt top with batting and backing; baste.
2. Outline quilt around the appliqué pieces, setting triangles, and borders. See the quilting suggestion below for the border and setting triangles.

3. Bind the edges with the 2"-wide green strips.
4. Add a label to the back of your finished quilt.

Broken Dishes Table Runner

The patchwork blocks in this table runner are a traditional pattern known as Broken Dishes. This project teaches you how to stitch multiple-fabric borders with corner squares and bias binding.

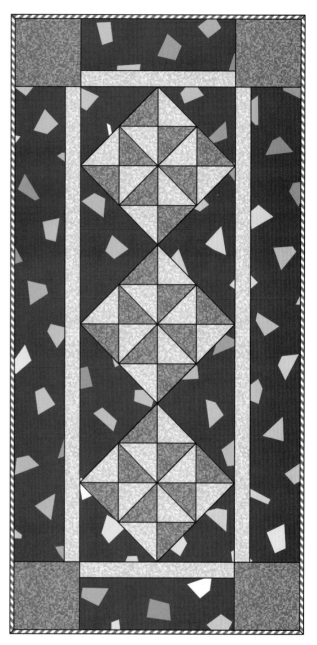

Color photo on page 44.

Project Information at a Glance	
Finished Table Runner Size:	19½" x 39½"
Name of Block:	Broken Dishes
Finished Block Size:	7"
Number of Blocks to Make:	3
Setting:	On Point
Border Treatment:	Multiple-Fabric Borders with Corner Squares
Finished Inner Border Width:	1"
Finished Outer Border Width:	3½"
Finished Corner Squares:	4½"
Binding:	Bias

Materials: 44"-wide fabric

1⅝ yds. teacup print for setting pieces, outer border, and backing

⅜ yd. yellow print for patchwork and inner border

⅜ yd. blue print for patchwork and corner squares

⅝ yd. striped fabric for bias binding

24" x 44" rectangle of low-loft batting

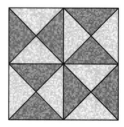

Cutting Setting Pieces and Borders

From the teacup print, cut:
  1 piece, 24" x 44", for backing
  2 strips, each 4" x 10½", for outer borders
  2 strips, each 4" x 30½", for outer borders
  1 square, 11¼" x 11¼"; cut the square twice
    diagonally for a total of 4 side setting
    triangles

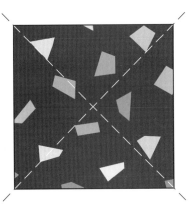

2 squares, each 5⅞" x 5⅞"; cut each square
  once diagonally for a total of 4 corner
  setting triangles

From the yellow print, cut:
  2 strips, each 1½" x 10½", for inner borders
  2 strips, each 1½" x 30½", for inner borders

From the blue print, cut:
  4 squares, each 5" x 5", for corner squares

From the striped fabric, cut:
  1 square, 20" x 20". Cut the square into bias
    strips, each 2" wide, following the direc-
    tions for cutting bias strips on page 32.

Cutting Block Pieces

Note: If you prefer to use a template to cut the patchwork pieces, turn to page 77.

Fabric	No. of Pieces	1st Cut	2nd Cut	Yield
Yellow	6	4¾" x 4¾"	⊠	24
Blue	6	4¾" x 4¾"	⊠	24

⊠ *Cut the squares twice diagonally.*

Block Assembly

The following directions are for making one Broken Dishes block. You can make one block at a time or all three blocks in assembly-line fashion.

1. Sew a blue triangle to a yellow triangle.

Make 8.

2. Join 2 units from step 1.

Make 4.

3. Join 2 units from step 2 to make a row.

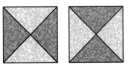 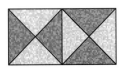

Make 2.

4. Sew 2 rows together to make a block.

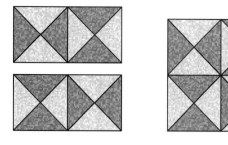

Table Runner Assembly

1. Arrange the patchwork blocks and setting triangles as shown. Sew the blocks, side setting triangles, and corner triangles 1 and 2 together in diagonal rows. Press the seam allowances toward the triangles.

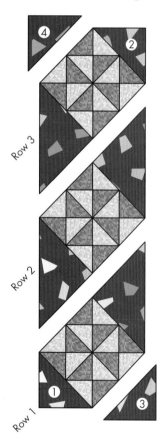

2. Sew the rows together. Add corner triangles 3 and 4 last.

3. Sew the 1½" x 30½" yellow border strips to the 4" x 30½" teacup border strips. Treat these as single borders and sew them to the long edges of the table runner.

Measure your runner through the center to determine the correct border lengths.

4. Sew the 1½" x 10½" yellow border strips to the 4" x 10½" teacup border strips. Treat these as single borders. Sew a blue corner square to each end of each border strip.

5. Sew the pieced borders to the short edges of the table runner.

Finishing

1. Layer the table runner with batting and backing; baste.
2. Outline quilt around the patchwork pieces, setting triangles, and borders. See the quilting suggestion below for the border and setting triangles.
3. Bind the edges with the 2"-wide bias strips.
4. Add a label to the back of your finished table runner.

Home Sweet Home

The Little House blocks in this quilt are fun to make, and they look great with a country checkerboard border. Repeating the blue fabric in the border unifies the quilt.

Color photo on page 41.

Materials: 44"-wide fabric

2¼ yds. tan print for patchwork, sashing strips, border, and backing
⅝ yd. red print for houses and binding
⅝ yd. blue print for house roofs and border
39" x 39" square of low-loft batting

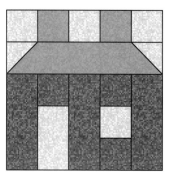

Project Information at a Glance	
Finished Quilt Size:	34½" x 34½"
Name of Block:	Little House
Finished Block Size:	10" x 10"
Number of Blocks to Make:	4
Setting:	Straight Set
Border Treatment:	Pieced Border
Finished Pieced Border Width:	4"
Binding:	Straight-Grain

Cutting Setting Pieces and Borders

From the tan print, cut:
1 piece, 39" x 39", for backing
2 strips, each 2½" x 10½", for sashing strips
3 strips, each 2½" x 22½", for sashing strips
2 strips, each 2½" x 26½", for sashing strips
4 strips, each 2½" x 40", for pieced border

From the red print, cut:
4 strips, each 2" x 40", for binding

From the blue print, cut:
4 strips, each 2½" x 40", for pieced border

Cutting Block Pieces

Note: If you prefer to use templates to cut the patchwork pieces, turn to page 79.

Fabric	No. of Pieces	Size to Cut	Placement
Tan	24 squares	2½" x 2½"	Background & window
	4 rectangles	2½" x 4½"	Doorway
Red	12 squares	2½" x 2½"	House
	12 rectangles	2½" x 6½"	House
Blue	8 squares	2½" x 2½"	Chimneys
	4 rectangles	2½" x 10½"	Roof

Block Assembly

The following directions are for making one Little House block. You can make one block at a time or all four blocks in assembly-line fashion.

1. With right sides together, place 1 tan square at each end of a blue rectangle. Use a pencil and ruler to draw diagonal lines on the squares as shown.

2. Sew on the drawn lines. Trim the excess fabric, leaving a ¼"-wide seam allowance. Press the triangles toward the corners. You have just made the roof.

3. Sew 3 tan squares and 2 blue squares into a row. These are the chimneys.

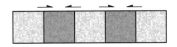

4. Sew the chimneys to the roof.

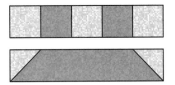

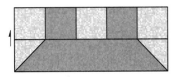

5. Sew a red square to a tan rectangle. This is the doorway.

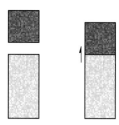

6. Sew a red square to each side of a tan square. This is the window.

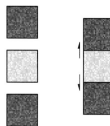

7. Arrange the units from steps 5 and 6 with 3 red rectangles to form the house. Sew these units together.

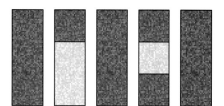

8. Sew the roof to the top of the house to complete your own Little House block.

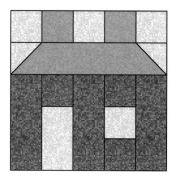

Quilt Assembly

1. Arrange the Little House blocks and the tan sashing strips as shown.

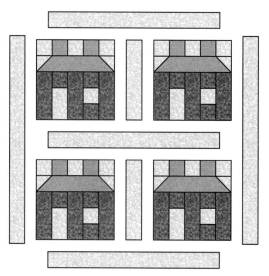

2. Sew the Little House blocks and the 2½" x 10½" sashing strips together to form 2 rows.

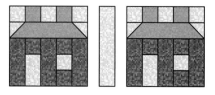

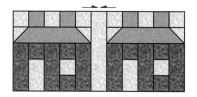

3. Sew the rows to the 2½" x 22½" sashing strips.

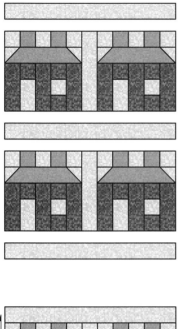

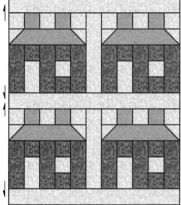

4. Sew the 2½ x 26½" sashing strips to opposite sides of the quilt top.

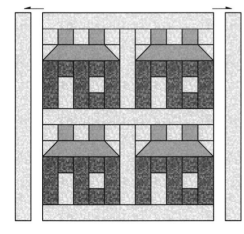

5. To make the pieced border, sew a 2½" x 40" tan strip to a 2½" x 40" blue strip.

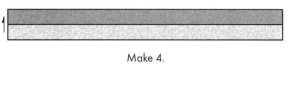

Make 4.

Press the seam allowances toward the blue strips on all of the strip sets. When you sew the units together, the seam allowances will lock and match perfectly!

6. Use a ruler and a rotary cutter to clean-cut the edges of the strip set. Cut a total of 16 segments from each strip set, each 2½ " wide.

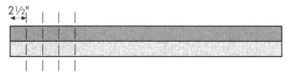

7. Sew 13 units together, reversing the tan and blue squares each time you sew.

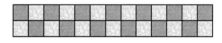

Make 2.

8. Sew these border units to opposite sides of the quilt top. Make sure that you place tan squares at the edges of the quilt top.

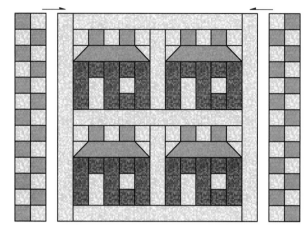

9. Sew 17 units together, reversing the tan and blue squares each time you sew. Make 2 border units. Sew these border units to the top and bottom of the quilt top, placing blue squares in the corners.

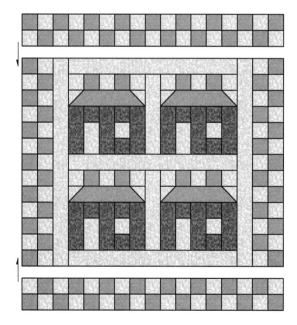

Finishing

1. Layer the quilt top with batting and backing; baste.
2. Outline quilt around the blocks. Machine quilt free-motion lines in the tan areas. Quilt diagonal lines through the pieced border.

3. Bind the edges with the 2"-wide red strips.
4. Add a label to the back of your finished quilt.

Holiday Nine Patch

The red-and-green color combination in this easy patchwork quilt is sure to brighten your holidays! The striped holiday fabric in the mitered border creates a fabulous finish.

Color photo on page 46.

Project Information at a Glance

Finished Quilt Size:	30" x 30"
Name of Block:	Nine Patch
Finished Block Size:	4½" x 4½"
Number of Blocks to Make:	13
Setting:	Straight Set with Alternate Squares
Border Treatment:	Mitered
Finished Inner Border Width:	½"
Finished Outer Border Width:	3"
Binding:	Straight-Grain

Materials: 44"-wide fabric

1⅝ yds. off-white print for patchwork blocks, alternate squares, and backing
½ yd. red print for patchwork blocks, inner border, and binding
1 yd. holiday-striped print for mitered borders
⅜ yd. green print for patchwork blocks
34" x 34" square of low-loft batting

Cutting Setting Pieces and Borders

From the off-white print, cut:
    1 piece, 34" x 34", for backing
    12 squares, each 5" x 5", for alternate squares

From the red print, cut:
    4 strips, each 1" x 34", for inner mitered
        border
    4 strips, each 2" x 40", for binding

From the holiday-striped print, cut:
    4 strips, each 3½" x 34", for outer mitered
        border

The design on your striped fabric may change the width of the borders in your quilt. That's fine, but they should be no wider than 4½". Cut the border strips carefully with scissors so that each strip contains the same design.

Cutting Block Pieces

Fabric	No. of Pieces	Size to Cut
Off-white	4	2" x 40" strip
Green	4	2" x 40" strip
Red	1	2" x 40" strip

Block Assembly

The following directions are for the strip-piecing method. You will make all 13 blocks at once.

1. Sew a 2"-wide green print strip to each long edge of a 2"-wide off-white print strip. Make an additional strip set. Use a ruler and rotary cutter to clean-cut the edges of the strip sets. Cut a total of 26 segments, each 2" wide.

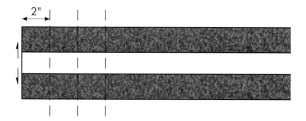

2. Sew a 2"-wide off-white print strip to each long edge of a 2"-wide red print strip. Use a ruler and rotary cutter to clean-cut the edges of the strip set. Cut a total of 13 segments, each 2" wide.

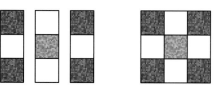

3. Join 2 green segments from step 1 and 1 red segment from step 2 to complete a block.

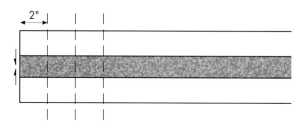

Make 13.

Quilt Assembly

1. Arrange the Nine Patch blocks and the alternate off-white print squares as shown.

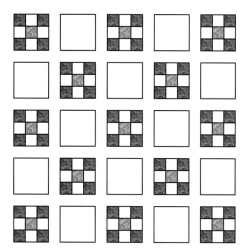

2. Join the blocks into 5 rows.

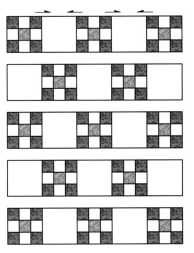

3. Join the rows to make the patchwork section of the quilt.

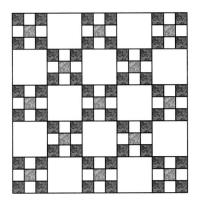

4. Sew the 1" x 34" red strips to the 3½" x 34" holiday-striped strips. Treat these as single borders.

Make 4.

5. Refer to pages 17–19 to add mitered borders to the patchwork section of the quilt.

Finishing

1. Layer the quilt top with batting and backing; baste.

2. Quilt through the centers of the green and red Nine Patch blocks. Outline quilt around the inner border and in selected stripes in the outer border. See the quilting suggestion below for the alternate squares. The quilting template is on page 78.

3. Bind the edges with the 2"-wide red strips.

4. Add a label to the back of your finished quilt.

Sparkles

Bright rainbow colors make these pinwheels a delight to sew! The pinwheel colors are repeated in the scrappy patchwork inner border and the pieced binding.

Color photo on page 45.

Project Information at a Glance	
Finished Quilt Size:	37" x 37"
Name of Block:	Pinwheel
Finished Block Size:	6" x 6"
Number of Blocks to Make:	9
Setting:	Straight Set with Sashing
Finished Sashing Width:	1½" and 2¼"
Border Treatment:	Scrappy
Finished Inner Border Width:	1½"
Finished Outer Border Width:	4"
Binding:	Scrappy

Materials: 44"-wide fabric

1¼ yds. black solid fabric for patchwork squares, sashing strips, and outer borders

¼ yd. each of 9 bright prints* for patchwork blocks, inner border, and binding

1¼ yds. multicolored print for backing

41" x 41" square of low-loft batting

Purple, gold, aqua, pink, yellow, red, green, orange, and blue

Cutting Setting Pieces and Borders

From the black solid fabric, cut:
- 2 strips, each 4½" x 29", for outer borders
- 2 strips, each 4½" x 37", for outer borders
- 6 strips, each 2" x 6½", for sashing strips
- 2 strips, each 2" x 21½", for sashing strips
- 2 strips, each 2¾" x 21½", for sashing strips
- 2 strips, each 2¾" x 26", for sashing strips

From each of the 9 bright colors, cut:
- 1 strip, 2" x 20", for inner scrappy pieced border
- 1 strip, 2" x 32", for binding

From the multicolored print, cut:
- 1 square, 41" x 41", for backing

Cutting Block Pieces

Note: If you prefer to use a template to cut the block pieces, turn to page 77.

Fabric	No. of Pieces	1st Cut	2nd Cut	Yield
Black	18	3⅞" x 3⅞"		36
Each bright print	2	3⅞" x 3⅞"		4

 Cut the squares once diagonally.

Block Assembly

The following directions are for making one purple Pinwheel block. Use a different color for each Pinwheel block and make nine blocks total.

1. Sew a purple triangle and a black triangle together. Make 4 units.

Make 4.

2. Arrange the 4 units so that the purple triangles form a pinwheel. Sew 2 units together to form 2 rows.

Make 2.

3. Sew 2 rows together to make the Pinwheel block.

Quilt Assembly

1. Arrange the Pinwheel blocks and 2" x 6½" black sashing strips as shown.

2. Sew the Pinwheel blocks and black sashing strips together to form 3 rows.

3. Sew the rows to the 2" x 21½" black sashing strips to make the patchwork section of the quilt.

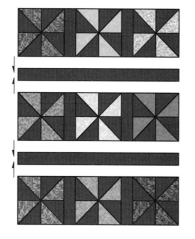

4. Sew the 2¾" x 21½" black strips to opposite sides of the quilt top. Sew the 2¾" x 26" black strips to the top and bottom edges of the quilt top.

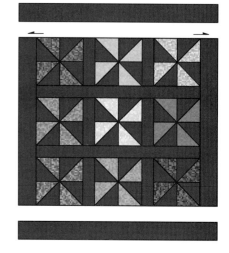

5. Sew the 2" x 20" strips of the 9 bright colors together in the following order: yellow, gold, orange, red, pink, purple, blue, aqua, and green. Use a ruler and rotary cutter to clean-cut the edges of the strip set. Cut a total of 8 segments, each 2" wide.

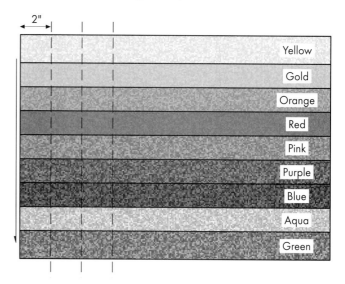

6. Sew 2 segments together, attaching a green square to a yellow square.

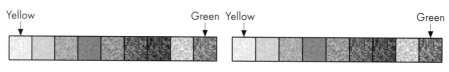

Make 4.

7. Use a seam ripper to remove the yellow squares at the ends of 2 strips. Save the squares!

8. Sew these shorter strips to opposite sides of the quilt top.

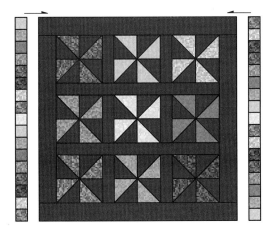

9. Sew a yellow square to the green square of each remaining strip. Press the seam allowance toward the yellow square. Sew these longer strips to the top and bottom of the quilt top.

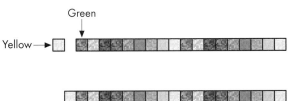

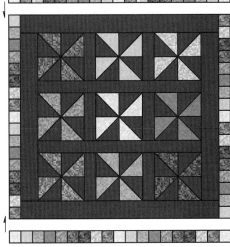

10. Sew the 4½" x 29" black border strips to opposite sides of the quilt top. Sew the 4½" x 37" black border strips to the top and bottom edges of the quilt top.

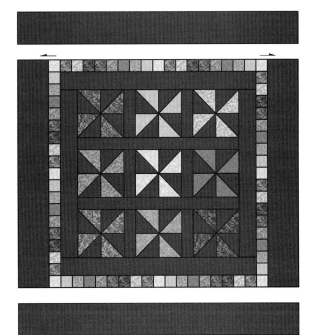

Finishing

1. Layer the quilt top with batting and backing; baste.

2. Outline quilt around the pinwheel patchwork pieces and the blocks. Outline quilt on either side of the scrappy patchwork border. See the quilting suggestion below for the outer borders.

3. Sew the 2" x 32" binding strips together to make a strip set. Use a short stitch length (20 stitches per inch); the small stitches will hold the little pieces securely when you crosscut the strips. Press the seam allowances open to distribute the thickness of the seams along the binding edge.

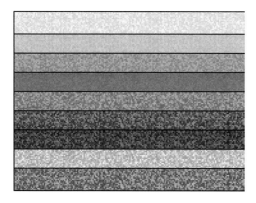

For future quilts, you can cut the strips in a variety of widths, or keep them a consistent width that relates to the sizes of the pieces in your quilt.

4. Use a ruler and rotary cutter to clean-cut the edges of the strip set. Crosscut the strip set into 12 segments, each 2¼" wide. (I cut pieced binding strips ¼" wider than usual to allow for the thickness of the seams around the quilt edge.)

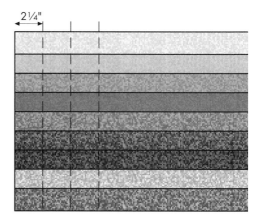

5. Sew the segments together to make enough binding to go around the perimeter of the quilt plus 10".

6. Fold the binding strip in half lengthwise, wrong sides together, and press with a hot steam iron.

7. Sew the binding to your quilt. (See page 28 for complete directions). If there is a binding seam near the corner miter fold, ignore it. It will be bulky, but it is not a problem.

8. Join the ends using the straight-and-easy connection (page 31).

9. Add a label to the back of your finished quilt.

Suggested Books

General Quiltmaking Techniques

Basic Quiltmaking Techniques for Strip Piecing by Paulette Peters (Martingale & Company)

Basic Quiltmaking Techniques for Divided Circles by Sherry Reis (Martingale & Company)

Basic Quiltmaking Techniques for Machine Appliqué by Maurine Noble (Martingale & Company)

Your First Quilt Book (or it should be!) by Carol Doak (That Patchwork Place)

The Joy of Quilting by Joan Hanson and Mary Hickey (That Patchwork Place)

Appliqué

Basic Quiltmaking Techniques for Hand Appliqué by Mimi Dietrich (Martingale & Company)

The Easy Art of Appliqué: Techniques for Hand, Machine, and Fusible Appliqué by Mimi Dietrich and Roxi Eppler (That Patchwork Place)

Hand Quilting

How to Improve Your Quilting Stitch by Ami Simms (Mallery Press)

Loving Stitches by Jeana Kimball (That Patchwork Place)

Border Treatments

Borders by Design by Paulette Peters (That Patchwork Place)

The Border Workbook by Janet Kime (That Patchwork Place)

Bindings and Edge Treatments

Happy Endings: Finishing the Edges of Your Quilt by Mimi Dietrich (That Patchwork Place)

A Fine Finish: New Bindings for Award-Winning Quilts by Cody Mazuran (That Patchwork Place)

Mail-Order Shopping

I hope you have a great quilt shop nearby. If not, mail-order catalogs are wonderful sources for the quilting supplies you need.

Clotilde, Inc.
Highway 54 West
Louisiana, MO 63353
1-800-772-2891
Fax: (954) 493-8950
Foreign Orders: (954) 491-2889

Keepsake Quilting
Route 25B
PO Box 1618
Centre Harbor, NH 03226-1618
1-800-865-9458
Fax: (603) 253-8346
Foreign Orders: (603) 253-8731

Quilts and Other Comforts
PO Box 2500
Louisiana, MO 63353
1-800-881-6624
Fax: 1-888-886-7196

About the Author

Mimi Dietrich lives with her husband and two sons in Baltimore, Maryland. She is a member of the Baltimore Heritage Quilters Guild and is a "founding mother" of the Village Quilters in Catonsville, Maryland, and the Baltimore Appliqué Society. She quilts on Monday nights with Monday Night Madness and on Fridays with the Catonsville Quilt and Tea Society.

Other books by Mimi Dietrich

Baltimore Bouquets

*Basic Quiltmaking Techniques
for Hand Appliqué*

*The Easy Art of Appliqué: Techniques for Hand,
Machine, and Fusible Appliqué*
(with Roxi Eppler)

*Happy Endings: Finishing the
Edges of Your Quilt*

*Quilts from the Smithsonian:
12 Designs Inspired by the Textile Collection
of the National Museum of American History*

Quilts: An American Legacy

Templates

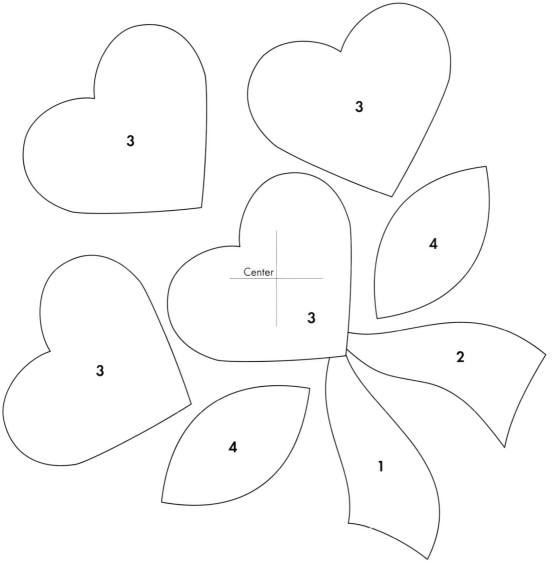

Center

Sweet Hearts
Appliqué Templates and Placement Guide

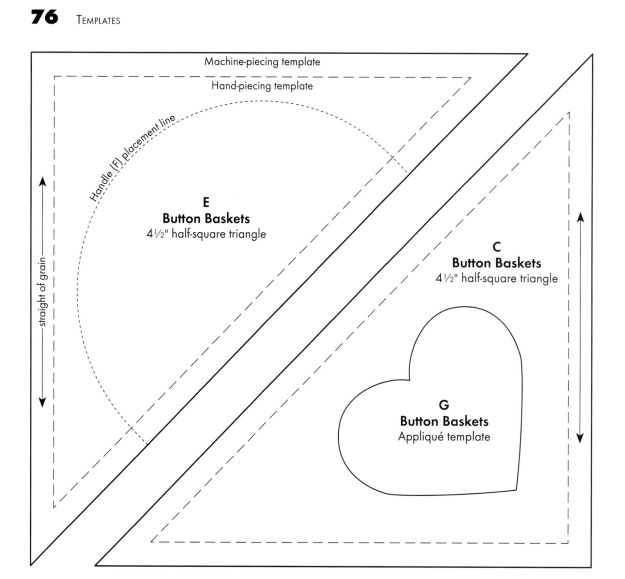

Machine-piecing template

Hand-piecing template

Handle (F) placement line

straight of grain

E
Button Baskets
4½" half-square triangle

C
Button Baskets
4½" half-square triangle

G
Button Baskets
Appliqué template

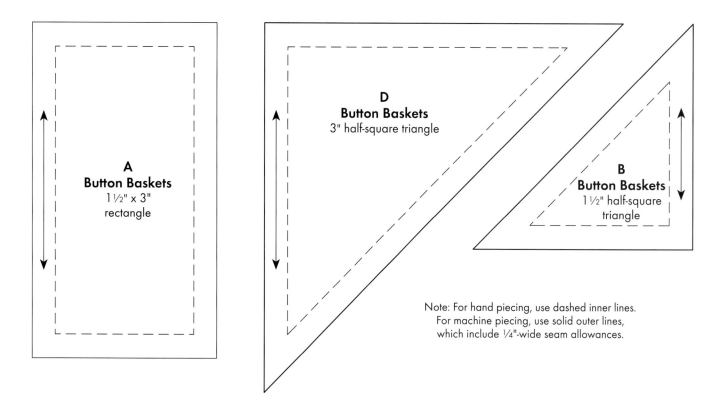

A
Button Baskets
1½" x 3"
rectangle

D
Button Baskets
3" half-square triangle

B
Button Baskets
1½" half-square
triangle

Note: For hand piecing, use dashed inner lines.
For machine piecing, use solid outer lines,
which include ¼"-wide seam allowances.

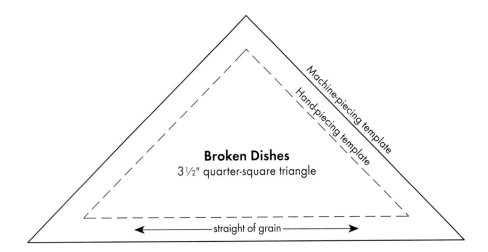

Broken Dishes
3½" quarter-square triangle

Machine-piecing template

Hand-piecing template

←———— straight of grain ————→

Note: For hand piecing, use dashed inner lines.
For machine piecing, use solid outer lines,
which include ¼"-wide seam allowances.

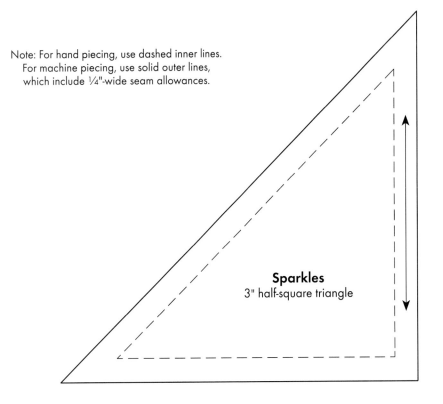

Sparkles
3" half-square triangle

Holiday Nine Patch
Quilting Template

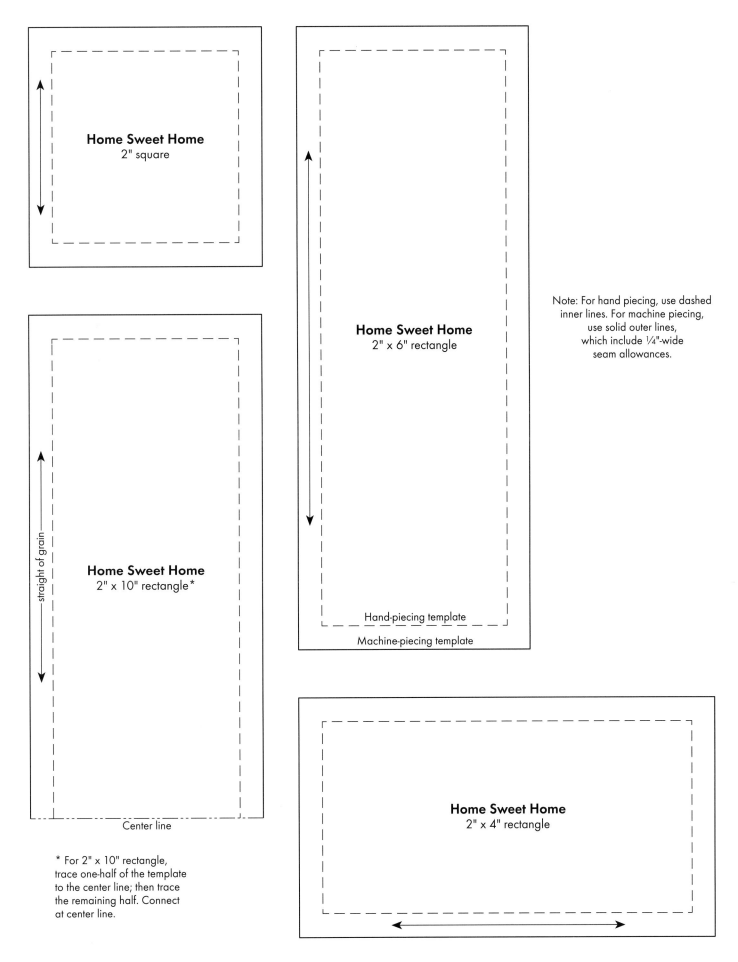

Home Sweet Home
2" square

Home Sweet Home
2" x 6" rectangle

Note: For hand piecing, use dashed inner lines. For machine piecing, use solid outer lines, which include ¼"-wide seam allowances.

straight of grain

Home Sweet Home
2" x 10" rectangle*

Hand-piecing template

Machine-piecing template

Center line

* For 2" x 10" rectangle, trace one-half of the template to the center line; then trace the remaining half. Connect at center line.

Home Sweet Home
2" x 4" rectangle

Books from Martingale & Company

Appliqué
Appliqué in Bloom
Baltimore Bouquets
Basic Quiltmaking Techniques for Hand Appliqué
Basic Quiltmaking Techniques for Machine Appliqué
Coxcomb Quilt
The Easy Art of Appliqué
Folk Art Animals
From a Quilter's Garden
Fun with Sunbonnet Sue
Garden Appliqué
Interlacing Borders
Once Upon a Quilt
Stars in the Garden
Sunbonnet Sue All Through the Year
Welcome to the North Pole

Basic Quiltmaking Techniques
Basic Quiltmaking Techniques for Borders & Bindings
Basic Quiltmaking Techniques for Curved Piecing
Basic Quiltmaking Techniques for Divided Circles
Basic Quiltmaking Techniques for Eight-Pointed Stars
Basic Quiltmaking Techniques for Hand Appliqué
Basic Quiltmaking Techniques for Machine Appliqué
Basic Quiltmaking Techniques for Strip Piecing
Your First Quilt Book (or it should be!)

Crafts
15 Beads
The Art of Handmade Paper and Collage
Christmas Ribbonry
Fabric Mosaics
Folded Fabric Fun
Hand-Stitched Samplers from I Done My Best
The Home Decorator's Stamping Book
Making Memories
A Passion for Ribbonry
Stamp with Style

Design Reference
Color: The Quilter's Guide
Design Essentials: The Quilter's Guide
Design Your Own Quilts
The Nature of Design
QuiltSkills
Surprising Designs from Traditional Quilt Blocks

Foundation/Paper Piecing
Classic Quilts with Precise Foundation Piecing
Crazy but Pieceable
Easy Machine Paper Piecing
Easy Mix & Match Machine Paper Piecing
Easy Paper-Pieced Keepsake Quilts
Easy Paper-Pieced Miniatures
Easy Reversible Vests
Go Wild with Quilts
Go Wild with Quilts—Again!
It's Raining Cats & Dogs
Mariner's Medallion
Paper Piecing the Seasons
A Quilter's Ark
Sewing on the Line
Show Me How to Paper Piece

Home Decorating
Decorate with Quilts & Collections
The Home Decorator's Stamping Book
Living with Little Quilts
Make Room for Quilts
Special-Occasion Table Runners
Stitch & Stencil
Welcome Home: Debbie Mumm
Welcome Home: Kaffe Fassett

Joy of Quilting Series
Borders by Design
The Easy Art of Appliqué
A Fine Finish

Hand-Dyed Fabric Made Easy
Happy Endings
Loving Stitches
Machine Quilting Made Easy
A Perfect Match
Press for Success
Sensational Settings
Shortcuts
The Ultimate Book of Quilt Labels

Knitting
Simply Beautiful Sweaters
Two Sticks and a String
Welcome Home: Kaffe Fassett

Machine Quilting/Sewing
Machine Needlelace
Machine Quilting Made Easy
Machine Quilting with Decorative Threads
Quilting Makes the Quilt
Thread Magic
Threadplay

Miniature/Small Quilts
Celebrate! with Little Quilts
Crazy but Pieceable
Easy Paper-Pieced Miniatures
Fun with Miniature Log Cabin Blocks
Little Quilts All Through the House
Living with Little Quilts
Miniature Baltimore Album Quilts
Small Quilts Made Easy
Small Wonders

Quilting/Finishing Techniques
Borders by Design
The Border Workbook
A Fine Finish
Happy Endings
Interlacing Borders
Loving Stitches
Quilt It!
Quilting Design Sourcebook
Quilting Makes the Quilt
Traditional Quilts with Painless Borders
The Ultimate Book of Quilt Labels

Rotary Cutting/Speed Piecing
101 Fabulous Rotary-Cut Quilts
All-Star Sampler
Around the Block with Judy Hopkins
Bargello Quilts
Basic Quiltmaking Techniques for Strip Piecing
Block by Block
Easy Seasonal Wall Quilts
Easy Star Sampler
Fat Quarter Quilts
The Heirloom Quilt
The Joy of Quilting
More Quilts for Baby
More Strip-Pieced Watercolor Magic
A New Slant on Bargello Quilts
A New Twist on Triangles
Patchwork Pantry
Quilters on the Go
Quilting Up a Storm
Quilts for Baby
Quilts from Aunt Amy
ScrapMania
Simply Scrappy Quilts
Square Dance
Strip-Pieced Watercolor Magic
Stripples Strikes Again!
Strips That Sizzle
Two-Color Quilts

Seasonal Projects
Christmas Ribbonry
Easy Seasonal Wall Quilts

Folded Fabric Fun
Holiday Happenings
Quilted for Christmas
Quilted for Christmas, Book III
Quilted for Christmas, Book IV
A Silk-Ribbon Album
Welcome to the North Pole

Stitchery/Needle Arts
Christmas Ribbonry
Crazy Rags
Hand-Stitched Samplers from I Done My Best
Machine Needlelace
Miniature Baltimore Album Quilts
A Passion for Ribbonry
A Silk-Ribbon Album
Victorian Elegance

Surface Design/Fabric Manipulation
15 Beads
The Art of Handmade Paper and Collage
Complex Cloth
Creative Marbling on Fabric
Dyes & Paints
Hand-Dyed Fabric Made Easy
Jazz It Up

Theme Quilts
The Cat's Meow
Everyday Angels in Extraordinary Quilts
Fabric Collage Quilts
Fabric Mosaics
Folded Fabric Fun
Folk Art Quilts
Honoring the Seasons
It's Raining Cats & Dogs
Life in the Country with Country Threads
Making Memories
More Quilts for Baby
The Nursery Rhyme Quilt
Once Upon a Quilt
Patchwork Pantry
Quilted Landscapes
Quilting Your Memories
Quilts for Baby
Quilts from Nature
Through the Window and Beyond
Two-Color Quilts

Watercolor Quilts
More Strip-Pieced Watercolor Magic
Strip-Pieced Watercolor Magic
Watercolor Impressions
Watercolor Quilts

Wearables
Crazy Rags
Dress Daze
Easy Reversible Vests
Jacket Jazz Encore
Just Like Mommy
Variations in Chenille

Many of these books are available through your local quilt, fabric, craft-supply, or art-supply store. For more information, call, write, fax, or e-mail for our free full-color catalog.

Martingale & Company
PO Box 118
Bothell, WA 98041-0118 USA

1-800-426-3126
International: 1-425-483-3313
24-Hour Fax: 1-425-486-7596
Web site: www.patchwork.com
E-mail: info@martingale-pub.com

3/99